Endorsement for *Fat Chance*

Fat Chance is a forensic autopsy of fate. Or, it is a violently controlled jeremiad against violence—where the pity is in the violence. So deeply disturbing, so bitten-back and wild, so unlike anything else, Kent MacCarter's *Fat Chance* is hard to categorise—and unforgettable.
Lisa Gorton

Fat Chance

Kent MacCarter

Kent MacCarter is a poet and publisher based in Castlemaine, Victoria. His publishing career began at University of Chicago Press in 2000; since then, he has worked with educational publishers and, for the past 12 years been the managing editor of Cordite Poetry Review and for 8 years publisher of Cordite Books. His writing has been published widely and includes four poetry collections. Kent has been an active participant in writing and publishing communities for decades.

Kent MacCarter

Fat Chance

Journalism Poems

First published in Australia in 2024
by Upswell Publishing
Perth, Western Australia
upswellpublishing.com

Upswell operates in the city of Perth, on ancient country of the Whadjuk people of the Noongar nation who remain the spiritual and cultural custodians of this beautiful land. We acknowledge their continuing connection to country and express gratitude to elders past and present for their strength and creativity...Always was, always will be, Aboriginal land.

ISBN: 978-0-6455368-8-1

A catalogue record for this
book is available from the
National Library of Australia

Cover design by Chil3, Fremantle
Typeset in Foundry Origin by Lasertype
Printed by McPherson's Printing Group

Upswell Publishing is assisted by the State of Western Australia through its funding program for arts and culture.

Department of
Local Government, Sport
and Cultural Industries

For those who didn't

Contents

Introduction 11

Fat Chance 15

Gossypiboma 67

California 91

Case Study 103

Epilogue 119

Acknowledgements 123

Introduction

The idiomatic expression 'fat chance' means 'very little or no possibility'. It's not quite *no* chance; there's still *a* chance, if only a slim one. The pieces in Kent MacCarter's *Fat Chance* are bound together by this sense of unlikely happenings – they recount tales of miraculous human and non-human survival, alongside stories of horrific, exotic demise as well as science, memoir and archives. Columns of justified prose help to lure us into the terrain of journalistic fact; we could be mistaken for believing there is no poet or poetry here at all.

And yet, this is not writing whose primary purpose is the transmission of facts. It is, rather, a book of 'journalism poems' – itself somewhat of an oxymoron. While journalism invests in the game of informational language, poetry resists such representation. It concerns itself less with what is said than with *how* it is said, drawing us into a spatio-temporal experience of and with the multiplicities of language and its affects.

MacCarter's 'journalism poems' (his term) might be considered a type of documentary poetry, a niche genre in which poets use documents and accounts to inform their poems, and use poetry as a tool with which to handle those documents. Poet and scholar Cole Swensen argues that the value of documentary poetry lies in its ability to 'incite the imagination of the reader', to push them 'beyond simply absorbing facts and into a responsive engagement with them because that engagement is a crucial part of truth. It's the emotional part, which can't be told; it must be felt'. But there are a variety of approaches to the crafting of documentary poetry, a 'continuum', as poet Mark Nowak puts it, 'from the first person auto-ethnographic mode of inscription to a more objective third person documentarian tendency'.

Fat Chance finds its place at the objective end of the continuum and demonstrates similarities to such works as Charles Reznikoff's *Holocaust*, M. NourbeSe Philip's *Zong!* or Nowak's own *Coal Mountain Elementary*. As with these works, MacCarter's subjective persona is deceptively absent. I say *deceptively* absent because the poet as a creative force is very much at work in the handling of this information – that is, in the selection, curation and presentation of the documentary materials *as poetry*, and in combination with the uses of poetic techniques such as juxtaposition, line breaks and the interplay between space and text. In contrast to conventional reportage, where the intention is to convey factual information to a relatively passive readership, the documentary poet's deliberate creative decisions provide a situation in which readers are invited to participate actively in meaning-making. They can readily identify such things as irony, absurdity and horror through the connections between unconnected things.

Because poetry already generates active readerships, documentary poetry bears the potential to be a site for an overt activist poetics. In the above-mentioned books, Reznikoff uses material from the Nuremberg Military Tribunal and Eichmann trials to confront the horrors of genocide; Philip exhumes and interrogates the historical massacre of enslaved Africans aboard the British slave ship *Zong*; and Nowak highlights the traumas and human costs associated with coal mining. MacCarter's *Fat Chance*, however, does not make such an explicit politicised demand. Rather, these poems seem to centre not on human virtue, or even human value, but on human folly.

Reading this book is like slowing down when driving past a car crash, not necessarily out of a sense of duty, or care, but as a way to see better. To commute from witnessing a horrible thing to *seeing* that horrible thing and, in so doing, forcing readers to flinch and respond in ways unique to themselves. MacCarter, as poet-reporter, does not shy away from explicit content, as if he wants us to be repulsed, disgusted, shocked; to understand the hazardous terrain beyond poetry's trade in beauty, safety and polish; even to question the noble cause of much documentary poetry.

Many of these pieces push at the edges of journalism – for one thing, these news stories are from the past, both distant and recent. Yet, there is an element of the new in MacCarter's colliding of facts that are far-flung and seemingly unrelated. Facts attract other facts, challenging journalism's confined narrative field. Where the first section of *Fat Chance* focuses on sole survivors of major airline crashes, the remaining sections of the book are somewhat less gruesome in detail, if sometimes gory.

This provides some relief, yes, although as 'journalism poems' they continue to provoke our readerly sensibilities in other novel ways. In another section, MacCarter activates a kind of reverse ekphrasis, deploying real history, dates and detail in the service of believability; in these pieces, journalistic narrative is completely abstracted so that we are left with spare flashes of the poet's encounters with historical material even where archival images do not exist, but could. In contrast to his drawing together of factual details in the first section, these poems force us to draw our own connections between floating signifiers to create meaning that sensibly refers back to their titles and noted source materials. Later sections return us to prose narrative; less work is required to build a story here, and yet the text rigorously tests the journalism poem as a sturdy vehicle for fact.

Fat Chance thrives on contradiction; indeed, contrary to the colloquial meaning of the book's title, these journalism poems offer us *ample* possibility. In colliding the journalistic with the poetic, MacCarter liberates language from the fact so that we can wander in the wide, bountiful space in between.

Jessica L Wilkinson

Fat Chance

18 July 2011

Jim Dostal, a farmer in Hutchinson, Minnesota, mourned the death of his prize-winning pig, Corndog. 'Everybody's asked how he's doing and how long he's going to live,' Dostal said. 'Well, he died from the summer heat yesterday.' Corndog was 12 years old. He weighed 600 kilograms at his final weigh-in. For years, Corndog was a popular attraction at the McLeod County Fair for years and received special honours at the 2006 Minnesota State Fair for being the largest contestant boar. Ever. He weighed only 520 kilograms then.

12 May 2010

'Under the circumstances, Ruben is doing well. He sleeps a lot. Now and then he is awake and is alert,' relatives read in a statement about their nephew, Ruben van Assouw. 'We told him that his parents and brother are dead.' Afriqiyah Airways Airbus A330-202 passenger flight consisted primarily of Dutch tourists departing from Johannesburg.

At 6 a.m., Flight 771 met the tarmac at Tripoli International Airport with no reported problems. For reasons unknown, the fuselage shattered from nose to tail instead of properly braking, resulting in a complete loss of hull. This is rare for a 1-year-old aircraft. There was no conflagration, only craft disintegration.

From the wreckage, books, cushions and souvenirs from South Africa comprised the largest intact pieces of recovery evidence for Libyan emergency crews to collect. Metal shards that were once the aircraft were notably smaller, and with human remains smaller still.

The afternoon before the crash, Ruben blogged about the camping trip that took him, his brother Enzo and their parents through some of the world's most rugged wildernesses: South Africa's Mac Mac Falls, Kruger National Park, into Swaziland and on into Lesotho. Twenty forensic experts were flown in from the Netherlands and had marginal success in identifying the body parts of 104 humans. Dutch officials repatriated what remained of individuals as soon as each was identified, a process that required a month to complete.

The 105th and only other passenger on the flight suffered multiple leg fractures and significant loss of blood from the nose. The 9-year-old boy was found alive, alert and entangled in his crushed seat with his blood dripping into his mouth. The seat was discovered 500 metres from the nearest debris and jabbed into a sand dune as a beach umbrella might be.

This landing saved the seat and the boy from tumbling over a deep ravine fewer than 5 metres away. 'He's okay. He's not getting any worse,' said an orthopaedic specialist to media later that evening.

15 January 2007

Jennifer Strange was 1 of 18 people who entered the 'Hold Your Wee for a Nintendo Wii' competition held by KDND, an FM radio station in Sacramento, California.

The contestants were asked to drink as much water as they could without urinating in a bid to win a video game console. Jennifer drank 11 litres of water in 3 hours. As the contest progressed, a disc jockey at KDND asked a co-host, 'Can you get water poisoning?' 'Not with water,' the co-host replied. 'Your body is 98% water. Why can't you take in as much water as you want?' 'Maybe we should have researched this before,' the disc jockey said.

Jennifer Strange's daughter was 11 months old when her mother doubled over and collapsed after coming in a close second place. Water intoxication, the county coroner later confirmed.

Jennifer Strange won 2 movie tickets for her second-place effort, which her daughter and husband redeemed the following week.

Her husband Billy said of their daughter, 'In the brief amount of time she spent with Jen, she really picked up on a lot of her qualities.'

At 107.9 on the dial, the station was named The End, acknowledging the last band in the FM broadcasting range. Its format was contemporary pop and soul.

16 August 1987

Cecelia Cichan was recovered in her assigned seat. It was intact, unburnt and upright in the middle of Interstate 94. She was alert, conscious, still buckled and clutching *World Traveller*, Northwest Airlines' in-flight magazine, in her hands.

Cecelia's flight lifted off the runway at 170 knots and began rolling from side to side at just under 15 metres above Detroit Metropolitan Wayne County Airport, Michigan.

Both of the jet's engines stalled, causing the aircraft to spiral 40 degrees to the port side and bisect a flood-light pole near the end of the runway. This removed 6 metres of the port wing and ignited an internal jet fuel tank. The aircraft then counterrotated 90 degrees with its starboard wing penetrating the roof of an Avis car hire building and a display of Ford Bronco II SUVs.

This action severed an equal length of outer starboard wing, igniting it by the same means. With that counterforce, the aircraft inverted a full 180 degrees and flew 2 kilometres upside down above Middlebelt Road's evening traffic.

Fire billowed from both ends of the severed wings. The aircraft cambered downwards onto the road, striking 2 vehicles and decapitating both drivers, although this did not arrest the inertia that the aircraft had achieved during full rotation.

The aircraft rammed the support abutments of a railroad bridge spanning Middlebelt Road. This impact quartered the fuselage – further retarding its pace – and caused the quadrants to roll down the commuter beltway until they concurrently ricocheted off an Interstate 94 overpass. The remaining structural integrity collapsed into unrecognisable char.

Dental records were ineffective in the casualty identification process. Cecelia Cichan was 4 years old.

Of the 154 other passengers and crew the largest piece of human remains was half of a woman's palm with 3 fingers still attached. It was a DC-9-82 passenger jet.

15 July 1964

Methuselah is a Great Basin bristlecone pine tree. Prometheus was one. Methuselah is 4855 years old, the oldest single living tree – or organism of any kind – on Earth. It grows at an undisclosed location within Inyo County, California. Prometheus would have been 4876 this year – 20 years Methuselah's senior – were it not for Donald R Currey of Chapel Hill, North Carolina, graduate student and US Forest Service cadet.

Donald was gripped by the dendrochronology craze sweeping across the botanical sciences in the '60s. His life's mission was to study climate dynamics of the Little Ice Age, an era that spanned from 1300 to 1800. There was much excitement when Prometheus was discovered and named in 1963. Non-invasive core samples were ordered by the Forest Service; eagerly Currey volunteered to extract them. Currey was a novice user of the increment borer. He jammed and broke the instrument soon after his penetration of Prometheus.

Alibis diverge here.

Observers claimed that Currey browbeat a fellow researcher out of his issued increment borer and proceeded to break that tool just as quickly as he had broken his own. Other observers claim that he immediately became enraged after his first failed attempt to obtain a sample.

Currey exploded into a fitful rage of hatchet vees and curses as he felled Prometheus within 30 minutes. No onlookers interfered with the actions of the only professional woodsman on the scene.

Prometheus listed over until its trunk's xylem and phloem completely separated, dying instantly.

Soon after the felling, a local elementary school teacher reminded Currey that the Little Ice Age was only 600 years ago and that hundreds of other, far younger trees would have provided identical data and supported his zeal.

Sections of Prometheus were divvied up between various research institutes.

One section resides in a convention centre in Ely, Nevada, under a Plexiglas casing. Its dried mass is permanently on display next to slot machines that are tuned to pay out jackpots at a rate 3–5% greater than the Nevada Gaming Control Board requires for Las Vegas. Ely is the county seat of White Pine County, and its only incorporated city. Per capita, it has the highest recorded rate of on-site casino gaming aggression.

6 March 2003

An Air Algérie Boeing 737-200 passenger jet listing 103 people on its manifest crashed on take-off from Hadj Bey Akhamok Airport in Aguenar, Algeria. Flight 6289 was a frequently scheduled short hop from there and Algiers. Before the aircraft became airborne, its starboard engine exploded during maximum thrust rotation. This instigated a frantic discussion between the pilot, male, and the co-pilot, female, about what emergency steps to execute next.

The co-pilot ordered landing gear up. The pilot did not respond. Again, she ordered the same command. It was again met with silence. The remaining good engine could not overcompensate for the drag that occurs at take-off and stalled.

With the landing gear still down, the flight carrying Youcef Djillali nosedived into a rocky outcrop near the runway's end, obliterating the aircraft on impact. The elapsed flight time was less than 2 minutes and achieved 180 metres in height at its apogee.

Youcef, age 28, was an experienced soldier having been involved in numerous regional conflicts in Algeria. He was discovered pinned beneath four of the 102 bodies recovered from the wreckage. He suffered more damage from a collapsed rib cage and a swollen brain, due to the weight of the cadavers atop him, than he did from the crash and the fire.

The 1980s

It is also known as the sowbug.

Thermosphaeroma thermophilum, commonly known as the Socorro Isopod, is the scarcest of 500 known species of freshwater isopod. Their marine cousins are found in habitats worldwide. Isopods are miniature crustaceans with 7 pairs of legs and range in size from 300 micrometres to 50 centimetres. By the late '70s – millennia into its unique speciation – the Socorro Isopod's natural habitat became extinct before it did.

The species' survival was confined to a population just large enough to maintain natural selection among the specimens that colonised 2 concrete water storage tanks. The tanks were fed by the mineral-heavy, freshwater trickle of Sedillo Springs in New Mexico and circulated by a network of sluices and overflows running between them.

The Socorro Isopods' universe had been reduced to 50 square metres. It was listed as an endangered species in 1978.

The tanks supplied water to hoses belonging to the City of Socorro's municipal golf course, primarily used in the upkeep of putting greens. The green on the 12th hole, a par 5, is closest to the tanks. Golfers occasionally birdied the hole, but no eagles or double eagles are known to have been recorded.

The species evolved to exhibit extremely rapid growth rates of young. To augment the population's natural diet of microbes provided by the spring, the mature isopods subsisted from cannibalistic feeding frenzies on their young. This occurred whenever the species teetered too close to unsustainability and subsequent extinction. This growth and feeding cycle had been repeating for 300,000 to 400,000 years, first in the spring water, then only in the tanks.

By 1999, due to nearby soil erosion and the denuding of native vegetation, weeds invaded the springs, forming a mass underground root system and choking off the species' water and food supply.

That same year, vandals also dumped a stolen and stripped motor vehicle into 1 of the 2 tanks, with steel rust quickly contaminating the delicate pH balance of the stored water. The recovered vehicle was registered with Arizona vanity plates that numbered SHED3VL.

Two captive populations of Socorro Isopods currently exist at the Albuquerque Biological Park. There, it has been recorded that, since captivity, the body size of female Socorro Isopod in both controlled groups has rapidly evolved to much larger dimensions than any in the known fossil record.

30 June 2009

Yemenia Flight 626 from Paris, an Airbus A310-324, dove into the Indian Ocean off the coast of the Comoros archipelago after an aborted landing approach to Prince Said Ibrahim International Airport. It missed the runway, as well as landfall, by 1 kilometre.

At the time of the crash, a waxing half-moon set at 9.23 p.m. No solar or lunar illumination was visible, and a back-up runway was attempted due to 65 kph winds occurring at the time of approach. Later, no record could be found of any aircraft ever attempting to land on the designated runway.

Bahia Bakari, age 12, did not know how to swim. It was 1.32 a.m. at the time of impact. She clutched floating debris for 15 hours – kicking, paddling and eventually waving to a distant fishing boat, gaining its crew's attention at 4 p.m. that afternoon.

Her face displayed multiple bruises and her collarbone was free-floating within her body. Of the 153 bodies recovered, only Bahia's was complete.

Grande Comore Island, where Moroni is located, is a mountainous island with volcanic peaks that reach a maximum of 2361 metres in elevation, including the Karthala volcano. It was unusually active the day before the crash, creating an open mesoscale cell convection. As a result, the volcano likely disrupted the lower tropospheric wind flow with a strong and unpredictable sheer.

In a city emergency ward, Bahia's uncle Joseph told her that her mother was in the next room, and that she could see her soon.

The mother's corpse was located a few days later, drifting back towards Paris via Madagascar.

9 December 2005

A chicken carcass is disinfected. Then it is deboned and separated by robots. Meat is minced in hoppers, then forced under high pressure to pass through grates that reduce the matter into a paste. Sodium phosphate is added. A stamping machine creates the shaped foodstuff. The McNugget is battered, fried and boxed for shipping. Chicken skin is also an important ingredient. In 2022, a limited-edition 40-piece box was marketed on Valentine's Day supported by an 'I'm lovin you' promotional campaign.

Robert James Mauleverer Garnett, age 35, had recently separated from his wife. Together, they had a 4-year-old daughter. Coroner John Sampson recorded a verdict of accidental death. Robert was a manager at a McDonald's outlet in Lambeth, South London.

Robert had poached himself by zipping up in a rubber suit after ingesting an enormous amount of cocaine and other narcotics. His body temperature increased with great alacrity, causing his brain to swell. His intention in donning a gimp suit was to increase the intensity of his high, but the result was death by hyperthermia and by the concurrent process of cerebral oedema – excessive fluids on the brain that cause its structural implosion.

His internal body temperature peaked at 45 °C, exacerbated by a 90% diminished capacity to sweat out toxins and release body heat. Broiler chickens are harvested at age 40 to 50 days. The average lifespan of a chicken is 5 years old.

PC Lee Clement, first officer on the scene, said police received a call from Robert's sister, Fiona, on Sunday 11 December, as she was concerned her brother had not been seen since Friday. He was due at an extended family gathering on the night of his death. Describing the scene after he broke into Robert's flat, Detective Clement said: 'I could see the bedroom ahead of me with the door open. The scene appeared untidy. There was a double bed ahead of me and the room was in darkness.'

A large body was found lying on its back on the bed. Its knees were raised with both feet planted on the bed. Three Ziploc bags with powdery residue lay on the floor beside the body.

Cocaine and ketamine were found in Robert's blood; traces of morphine were found in his urine. Detective Sergeant Paul Byrne later told the inquest: 'There was no suggestion of third-party or criminal involvement'.

Big Macs differ in size, protein and fat quotients in each country they are served. In the UK, a Big Mac offers 2340 kilojoules of energy. They are pre-made and housed in air-tight steam trays, awaiting sale, assembly and consumption.

8 July 2003

The passenger manifest of Sudan Airways Flight 139 showed that 14 of its 117 passengers and crew were children, including 4 infants. Mohammed el-Fateh Osman was 2 years old when the Boeing 737 he was aboard crashed on its way from Port Sudan Airport to Khartoum.

The pilot reported an issue with the starboard engines 10 minutes before the crash, but did not extrapolate further detail. At the time, Sudan was 20 years into civil war. Flight 139 had just departed the country's only significant port – site of the state-owned oil complex and terminal of the main pipeline from Sudan's south-central oil fields.

Mohammed was the final person to be located in the wreckage, discovered due to a wailing cry not indicative of any native bird species recognisable to the emergency recovery crew. Qulai, a volunteer, found him wedged inside a food service trolley, where assorted fruits and packets of snacks provided a buffer to Mohammed's cranium against the impact.

One hundred and sixteen passengers' bodies were burned so extensively that the remains were buried immediately on-site in a mass grave. Repatriation was not an option. Fifteen per cent of Mohammed's skin was burned to the muscle, and he was missing his right leg from the kneecap down. He was airlifted to the UK for emergency treatment.

The trolley was lodged 8 metres up into a tree and was festooned with charred human epidermis. Sudan consumed 5300 barrels of refined jet fuel per day in 2013. The United States consumed 1,434,400 barrels.

Sheikh Zayed bin Sultan al-Nahyan, President of the United Arab Emirates at the time, funded Mohammed's medical treatment, and wealthy businessmen from Egypt funded his primary and secondary education thereafter.

At age 15, he was invited by the Saudi Commission for Tourism to journey to Makkah for Hajj. Said Mohammed, 'I never had the chance to come to Saudi Arabia before. People assume that I have a phobia of planes because of the crash, but I love being on airplanes and I don't remember it.'

Qulai, invited by Mohammed's father – who was not on the flight – to join his household in the UK soon after the crash, accompanied him on the journey. Before he recovered the child, Qulai had been displaced from his family property to make way for a new oil field.

Mustafa Osman Ismail, then Foreign Affairs Minister of Sudan, claimed that the United States' penalties imposed on Sudan in 1997 for alleged terrorist activity and sponsorship had created extensive goods shortages in Sudan, notably vital aircraft parts, fresh produce and crude oil.

15 February 2018

Grigore Bulbuc, age 31, an experienced tree surgeon from Romania, had just begun the prune of a tall, private-garden sycamore in the south-east London area of Bermondsey. A sapling of the same species was maturing, and it needed root space and air space for its habit and future canopy.

At around 11 a.m., the top-handled chainsaw he was working with kicked back from a routine cut, severed his right shoulder, removed his right arm, then passed through a neck artery and ground his left jugular vein as the blade slowed to an idle. This resulted in a catastrophic haemorrhage. He had largely decapitated himself.

Enough blood flow reached his brain from the remaining neck veins and tendons for Grigore to remain conscious for nearly an hour after the accident.

Charles Hurst, senior manager of Aralia Tree Services – handlers of saplings to old-growth timber – witnessed the chainsaw recoil into Grigore's neck and immediately attempted to scale the tree to help. His arborist was dangling 7 metres in the air at the end of a safety rope. The main sycamore trunk was slicked with enough blood that finding purchase on it with a climbing belt was nearly impossible.

The accident happened fewer than 10 metres away from local Southwark Park Primary School, where children were outside on recess and began to climb its boundary fence to better view an all but headless tradesman dangling from a rope with an idling chainsaw strapped to his left hand.

He had a 1-year-old son. Charles later recounted that Grigore shouted four words post-accident, 'I'm dead, I'm dead!' as he clutched at his neckline. Later, the attending coroner concluded that enough oxygen and nervous energy had remained in the nearly severed head to articulate this thought, power its enunciation and to potentially notice the children watching him pendulum as he did so. Charles cut Grigore from the safety rope, lowered him to the street, and talked him through remaining calm until the ambulance arrived.

Grigore had been a tree surgeon for 10 years, routinely handling chainsaws correctly. On this occasion, he errantly held the saw with only his left hand – in close proximity to his body – while cutting a major hardwood limb held by his right.

Charles later told the inquest that he saw Grigore as a genuine 'climber' in his tree surgery firm, that his future had been very bright and that his organisational chart would have a major hole in it that may never regrow. This accident occurred 1 week before Grigore's 32nd birthday.

18 May 2018

Flight 972 crashed at 12.08 p.m., fewer than 30 seconds after take-off. It immediately banked sharply to its port side over an open paddock.

Ten pastors and their wives from Havana's Church of the Nazarene were among the 113 passengers and crew that lifted off in a 39-year-old Boeing 737-201 Adv from Santiago de Las Vegas Airport, Cuba. Damojh LLC of Mexico City was the aircraft's fifth owner, subleasing the asset to Global Air, which subsequently hired it out to Cubana de Aviación for charter service. It was forbidden to enter US or Canadian airspace.

The flight recording began with cabin crew laughter and chatter about their previous night out. The pilot gave vessel command to the co-pilot, who was on his first service after a 5-year hiatus without interim training or practice.

'What did this guy do?' the captain is recorded inquiring. He took command of the craft, heaved the wheel to the left and righted the aircraft for 3 seconds. Banking occurred 5 times, each time more violently.

The aircraft pitched upwards, inverted, dropped, collided with a herd of dairy cattle, struck a farmhouse and then disintegrated along a railway line just as its twin engines were reaching maximum thrust with zero response from guidance systems. Four passengers survived the impact, with 2 living less than a week. Grettel Landrove, age 23, lived another 31 days.

Mailén Díaz Almaguer, age 19, found wrapped around a twisted rail line, was immediately transferred to Calixto García Hospital, where she spent the next 205 days. She did not have respiratory, pulmonary, urinary or digestive function on arrival and suffered paraplegic nerve damage.

Additional injuries included disfiguration of the spine, cervical collapse, compressed thoracic dorsal extremities, splintered tibia, fibula and pelvis, and gluteal burns that required constant draining.

An investigative committee found that the actual take-off weight far exceeded what was recorded and used in pre-flight calculations. The aircraft's centre of gravity was 10% further astern than the crew believed, exacerbating incorrect weight ratios to 29% greater than accounted for. Extreme banking would have caused enough centripetal force to pull passengers off their seats.

On her 20th birthday in December 2018, Mailén resumed social media by posting her first post-accident selfie on Facebook. Lenier Mesa, Cuban popstar, paid her a surprise hospital visit, presenting her with a statuette of St Francis of Assisi, patron saint of animals and environment, and a plush toy cow.

7 June 2016

When a Yellowstone National Park ranger crew returned the next day, they discovered that Colin Nathaniel Scott, age 23, of Portland, Oregon, had completely dissolved.

Wyoming's Norris Geyser Basin is the hottest, most active geothermal region in the park. Water temperature ranges from 80 to 237°C. Geysers are fed by underground water enriched with sulphuric acid.

Green, orange and lavender-coloured micro-organisms break down hydrogen sulphide found in minerals and soil. They ascend thermal currents to pool surfaces and cluster in pastel streaks with a pH value of 1.

Colin and his younger sister Sable breached a protected boardwalk and hiked 200 metres to bathe in thermal water, colloquially known as hot-potting.

Sable began filming her brother as he reached down to check the temperature of a pool 2 metres wide, 4 metres deep and what turned out to be 92°C. She captured Colin slipping and falling into the acid bath.

Calcified minerals rimming the pool were too brittle to assist him. Sable ran to the emergency phone at Porkchop Geyser to summon West District ranger Tara Ross, who responded immediately.

All geysers are fenced.

Hazard signage is visible from hiking trails, car parks and features on billboards throughout Yellowstone. Warnings appear on park-issued maps and are discussed in person as you enter the park.

Once Colin's apparel disintegrated, he went into immediate shock, with extreme universal pain. His nervous system no longer registered sensation after 1 minute. His epidermis, dermis and subcutis layers eroded completely.

Capillaries burst with full blood loss, muscle tissue terminated function and all subcutaneous fat boiled off. Universal organ failure occurred. Colin's skeletal structure fractured, and his bones began breaking down in the swirl of acidic solution. Sable resumed filming.

An emergency crew led by Deputy Chief Ranger Lorant Veress staged numerous attempts to enmesh Colin's remains from the hotpot's opaque water with long catch poles, but the location was precarious and a lightning storm was gathering. Recovery was suspended until dawn.

What remained of Colin was a melted orange flip-flop and a blackened wallet containing driver, hunting and fishing licences and a retailer rewards card.

The ASTM International Resin Identification Coding System lists the type of rubber used in the flip-flop's manufacture as 7 – a durable polymer that cannot be recycled.

22 July 1973

Pan Am Flight 816 radioed to Fa'a'ā International Airport in Papeete, Tahiti, requesting emergency landing procedures due to the Boeing 707-321B's windshield sustaining a crack during its flight from Auckland. It made a routine landing.

Passengers were informed that layover time in Papeete was extended – enough to replace all windshield panels – and that they could disembark and clear customs for a seafood dinner if desired. They were not given a reason for the extension. The name painted on the aircraft read *Clipper Winged Racer.*

With its windshield replaced, the aircraft took off at 10.06 p.m. on a maximum-fuel, non-stop flight to Los Angeles. A Pan American World Airways representative later stated that the crew had not radioed any indication of trouble to the Papeete control tower during take-off and early ascent.

Pierre Angeli, then Governor of French Polynesia, accompanied by attaché Aymar Achille-Fould, Secretary of the French Defence Ministry, were transported to the marine crash site aboard a small government vessel 5 kilometres north of Papeete Harbour. Secretary Achille-Fould was in Tahiti for nuclear warhead testing that was routinely occurring on outer keys of the archipelago. 'All Tahiti is in consternation,' he was quoted saying of the crash.

The site was strewn with clothes, hair, seat upholstery, wires and human tendons, entangling the propellers of the first rescue boats and Governor Angeli's craft. A fleet of private yachts set out, trailing New Zealand Navy tugs, to search for passengers and to rescue the officials.

Ninety seconds after take-off, Papeete control tower received a call from the cockpit. No voices spoke. No distress was communicated by pilot Robert M Evarts of Grass Valley, California, age 59, who was on his 25,275th flight hour. The only sound was the catastrophic failure of the new windscreen panels that had been installed hours before. The plane entered the Pacific Ocean at an 87-degree angle where the Moorea Coral Reef ends and deeps begin.

Of 79 passengers and crew, 12 bodies were recovered. So too was James Neil Campbell, a Canadian travel agent who specialised in maritime holiday packages. The impact was so great that the remains of the other 66 passengers and crew were never located in the 1000-metre deep water.

The flight's black box was not recovered. Disintegration of the windshield panels likely caused a double gyro-horizon malfunction, thus retarding autopilot manoeuvres as well as the removal of the pilot's and co-pilot's heads from the glass shrapnel.

James awoke floating, buoyed by oil in brackish water. He could not discern up or down. Jet fuel congealed to his entire body. He suffered universal contusions but no broken bones or serious injury. He walked off the rescue boat upon its return, not knowing who he was or anything about his life before impact, and he never would again.

The 41st test ordered by Secretary Achille-Fould, codenamed Centaur, occurred over Mururoa Atoll on 17 July 1974. Its mushroom cloud drifted in an unexpected trajectory, exposing 110,000 people on Tahiti and the Windward Islands group – the entire population of French Polynesia – to extreme levels of ionising radiation. Sixty-three French Polynesian civilians received health compensation and additional fishing rights from the French Government.

26 November 2009

Undeterred, the family again crossed the Rio Grande and settled at 719 N 14th St in Council Bluffs, Iowa, in 2007. Larry Ely 'Marlon' Murillo-Moncada had a lean build: 183 cm tall and 63.5 kilograms in weight.

The No Frills Supermarket in Council Bluffs shuttered in late 2016. Its assets were liquidated, including a pair of walk-in coolers used to store perishables. They were 3.5 metres high, set 45 cm in front of the rear wall and were accessible to customers and to staff. Its final coupon insert in the local advertiser was for 30% off iceberg lettuce.

'It was a blizzard at the time,' Sergeant Brandon Danielson of the Council Bluffs Sheriff's Department stated. 'He left with no shoes, no socks, no keys, no car.'

Larry and his family were deported – on grounds of insufficient documentation – from their United States home back to Honduras when he was 8 years old. Calls were made. Fliers appeared around the city east of Omaha, Nebraska. Nine years passed. Frequent customer reports of odours were collected in the supermarket office.

Larry was reported missing the day after Thanksgiving. He left his parents' house upset after an argument, suffering hallucinations. He walked into the snow barefoot at 6.15 p.m. wearing a light-blue hoodie and trousers, and was never heard from again.

Ana Murillo-Moncada, Larry's mother, told the *Daily Nonpareil* that her son had come home after a shift and seemed disoriented. She took him to a doctor. There, he was prescribed antidepressants and anxiety medication to counter his deportation experience.

In depositions, former colleagues said that it was common for staff to crawl atop the coolers and eat expired food, Halloween candy, pet food on dares and off produce during breaks; a known refuge from the job and where a surreptitious smoke could be had.

'He said somebody was following him, and was scared,' said Ana. 'He was hearing voices that said … *eat sugar*. He felt his heart was beating too hard and thought if he ate sugar, his heart would not beat so hard.'

On 24 January 2019, contractors began to dismantle the coolers. They discovered a significantly decomposed corpse wedged behind them.

Larry walked back to work, scaled the coolers and fell into the narrow space between them and the wall. Refrigeration compression motors were on at all times. 'It's so loud, there's probably no way anyone heard him,' Sgt Danielson recounted. He died by dehydration after 5 days without being able to move and was discovered 10 years later.

Children aged 7 and 8 at a deportation facility in Clint, Texas, were found sleeping on concrete floors and denied soap and toothpaste. Many wore clothes sodden with blood, snot and tears. In 2019, 7 children died in US custody, compared with none in the 10 years prior.

Larry's body putrefied and dripped onto the floor, mistaken for other seepages in everyday usage of the coolers. Colleagues mopped him up, thinking him juice from spoiled fruit. His corpse ossified into a brittle crust around the coolers' air intake vent that helped keep its contents fresh.

Customers breathed in carbon dioxide emitted by Larry's decomposing remains while shopping. The customer base slowly dwindled.

'Our food ration was in quality a starving one, being either too foul to be touched or too raw to be digested.' This is a detainee recount from Andersonville Labor Camp in the Civil War-era state of Georgia 163 years earlier.

Larry was identified on 22 July 2019.

3 September 1997

There was no mention whether she had foreseen the crash. Vietnam Airlines Flight 815 departed Ho Chi Minh City at 1.07 p.m. on a 45-minute service to Pochentong International Airport in Phnom Penh. The 13-year-old Tupolev Tu-134B-3 aircraft began its approach in drizzle. The airport's 'very high frequency omni-directional range radar' had been looted the previous July by soldiers loyal to Cambodian coup d'état leader Hun Sen, and the back-up non-directional beacon (NDB) – a less sensitive instrument – was in force.

Looting of the crash site began immediately by military and police. Locals joined, taking watches from disembodied wrists and making off with smouldering steel panels. The Cambodian Government offered rewards for the flight recorder, the data recorder and the quick access recorder: acquired from looters for USD $10, $200 and $1500 respectively.

The aircraft had completed 8208 commercial flights in 11,722 flight hours without incident. A witness recounted seeing the aircraft aloft with multiple emergency doors open and could see passengers crowding the exits and looking for ground. None jumped.

Due to fixture looting, airport director Sok Sambour ruled that aircraft landing requests be set at 4300 metres. Captain Pham Van Tieu set it at 5000. Once within NDB range, Pham again requested to land at 1500 and 910 metres, stating no runway visual on both occasions. He was given permission to drop to 610 metres.

It was early afternoon with cloud cover down to 3 metres. Runway lights had been looted weeks earlier. American photojournalist David Longstreath was at the airport covering exiled King Norodom Sihanouk's return to Cambodia to re-sort relations with Khmer loyalist Lord Prime Minister Supreme Military Commander Hun Sen.

Flight 815 was sighted at 61 metres. First officer Hoang Van Dinh asked Pham to abort. Pham replied, 'Wait a little', descended to 30 metres, and asked crew to keep their eyes open. Hoang countered, 'Don't see, don't see, captain. Turn back!'

Although possessed by her goddess spirit, Sim Viklay, popular soothsayer at nearby Wat Kok Banh Chon, recounted to the *Phnom Penh Post* her and companion Ly Yen's eyewitness heroics. 'I heard the boy crying and saw him near the middle of the plane, lying on the ground by burning parts.'

Viklay sped her Honda Dream moto towards Kossamak Hospital while Yen rode pillion holding the bleeding but alive toddler in heavy rain.

Four seconds later the Tupolev's port wing struck a palm tree, shutting down 1 engine and igniting flames from the aircraft's tail. The starboard wing then sliced through an apartment building before striking ground at 270 kilometres per hour. It caromed 180 metres through rice paddies, decapitated 2 oxen and suffered a universal hull explosion at 1.40 p.m., obliterating 65 of the 66 people on board.

Although not a religious figurehead, Viklay performs at a well-known shrine in the wat. Wealthy Phnom Penhois queue to sit at her feet to hear her prophecies. Democide and human disappearances during King Sihanouk's reign number at least 3,151,000.

'I was dressed in black Levis and polo shirt. My Tony Lama snakeskin boots were spit-shined to a high gloss', said David.

He was able to breach the airport's emergency doors to get to the wreckage unrestrained, where he captured a newswire image of 14-month-old Thai national Chanayuth Nim-Anong mid-rescue. Nothing more is known about the boy.

26 March 2017

The most challenging part of swallowing Akbar whole, feet first, was manoeuvring its elasticated mandibles around his shoulder blades.

It's quite shy and typically preys on boars and wild dogs. No definitive evidence of its predation occurring existed, only an occasional binturong or sun bear. Said Akbar's neighbour, Satriawan, 'He was found in the location of the garden.'

Word spread. Crowds amassed, their cameras readied. The snake's muscle reflex remained inert when a local man beheaded it with a single chop from a 30 cm blade. Within 6 minutes, the reticulated python's (*Python reticulatus*) 7.2-metre body was flayed.

At dawn, Akbar Salubiro, a 25-year-old farmer, left his home, breakfast in hand, for the palm oil plantation where he worked in Central Mamuju Regency, West Sulawesi, Indonesia. It was a short walk, as he lived next door to it. His wife Munu and their 2 sons were away visiting her mother in another village. Co-workers reported him tardy for work.

First, a sensation like giving an impromptu piggyback ride. Then, with every exhalation from Akbar, the snake methodically exerted its 7.8 pounds per square inch of pressure on Akbar's circulatory system, backing up blood in his aortae until his heart burst in cardiac arrest and emptying his alveoli until asphyxiation.

The tropical biota of Indonesia has lost 0.84 mega hectares of primary forest and predator habitat per year since 2000, significantly outpacing deforestation rates in Brazil. Half of this is attributed to palm oil expansion – 50% of global consumption in 2017, representing AUD $38.7 billion in Indonesian exports that year. Around 7.2 million people rely on the industry for livelihood.

Salubiro's uncle was notified about the demerit, walked to his nephew's home and found it locked and empty. He convinced local police to issue a manhunt, which recovered a right-footed boot and harvesting tool from the immediate area.

Locals from Akbar Salubiro's namesake village spotted the misshapen python in an irrigation sluice on the plantation. It struggled with any rectilinear locomotion even when provoked, and 2 protuberances were discernible from its distended body.

Colleagues and village elders huddled over what to do, then voted to kill the python to confirm, or disprove, a niggling concern about its atypical behaviour.

Akbar was seconds outside of his home when the python, an ambush predator, lunged from an overhead tree and wrapped its length around him from kneecaps to sternum. After the boreal ecosystem, tropical forests are the largest terrestrial carbon sink on Earth, storing approximately 428 gigatonnes.

Earth's atmosphere stores 589. An adult reticulated python can exceed 200 kilograms in weight.

First, the left boot; then, 2 legs in trousers; digits clutching an unsmoked Gudang Garam cigarette and a box of Teh Kotak jasmine tea with straw still in its packaging; a shirted torso, then Akbar's head of matted hair were revealed and videoed.

'It's him,' said Mashura, another neighbour. *Tribun Timur* acquired his video and published it online, where it soon went viral. Salubiro Junaidi, village secretary, later recounted, 'People heard cries from the palm grove the night before Akbar was found'. Here, a single hectare of tropical rainforest harbours over 200 plant species and reliant herbivores.

More than 60% of omnivorous Indonesian rainforest species are endemic. Munu learned of her husband's death by watching regional news on television while eating snake bean salad.

24 December 1971

Remains of a LANSA Lockheed L-188A Electra turboprop sprinkled over the mountainous terrain near Puerto Inca, Peru, after a lightning strike caused its mid-air explosion. There had been very heavy turbulence and the plane was shimmying violently. Luggage, gifts, flowers and Christmas cake projectiles throughout the cabin caused the first casualties.

Electricity remaining in a fading tropical storm caused St Elmo's fire – a rare occurrence of a highly charged electrical halo that encapsulates conductive airborne objects. The starboard engine disintegrated.

Juliane Köpcke is a professor of biology in Germany. She was a 17-year-old girl flying with her mother to Lima. She found herself strapped into her seat, fully conscious and, at this point, uninjured, hurtling in a parabolic lob from the force of the detonation at 3500 metres above ground level.

'That is the end, it's all over.' Those were the final words Juliane heard from her mother. The plane stalled into a freefall nosedive and broke apart before hitting the jungle below. Her final thought before she passed out was that the rainforest resembled broccoli.

When she awoke, her seat was upright on the jungle floor with her still in it. It was 9 a.m. precisely. Her watch still worked.

Her arms and legs were slashed from branches and her collarbone was fractured. 'When I heard the sounds of running water, I knew I had to follow it because a river would lead to a human settlement,' she later recalled.

Juliane was wearing a short, sleeveless cotton mini-dress. One of her white sandals remained. Her vision was profoundly myopic, and her glasses had been blown off during her descent.

She used her remaining sandal to ascertain the ground ahead of her as she walked, checking for snakes, quicksand and bogs. She scooped maggots from her wounds, and then ate them. She drank mud.

On the third day of survival, she ran across a 3-seat row from the wreckage, upside down and staked half a metre above the ground. Supporting it were 3 bodies still buckled in, rammed into the earth headfirst up to their shoulders, feet sticking upwards. The heads had acted as arrowheads upon impact.

On day 10, Juliane followed a river and was found by lumbermen from a remote settlement. They first mistook her for a water goddess from tribal legend – a hybrid of a water dolphin and a blonde, white-skinned woman.

Two of the 92 passengers survived the explosion and the 3500-metre fall: Juliane and her mother. Fewer than half the bodies were recovered.

Her mother's body was discovered on 12 January 1972. The coroner concluded that she too had survived the fall impact but had been too badly injured to walk. She died by dehydration in the rainforest.

18 July 2011

'He had a pretty good temper,' Dostal reflected. 'He wasn't mean. Corndog always liked to be scratched on the neck, you know … I feel down in the dumps, but life goes on and I've got to take care of all my other animals.'

Gossypiboma

1.

Dear Santa Claus

Thank you for the electric train set and thank you for the new shirt. It is big and I have worn it 3 times. The Shazam comics is my favourite boxcar now in HO. The doors open and I put marshmallows and tinsel and light bulbs inside.

Retained surgical bodies (RSB) are any foreign bodies left inside the patient after the operation … The consequence of foreign bodies after surgery may manifest in different forms immediately after the operation, months or … years after the procedure … The risk of retained surgical bodies [is] *complicated* [in] *cases* [with] *obese patients or trauma requiring the use of numerous instruments, retractors and surgical sponges.*

The Chattanooga Choo Choo has electric smoke and it came from Florida. I pretend that Xmas light bulbs are people and I like the red and blue and yellow ones the best. The snowbanks are big outside and my sled is underneath them.

If patients complain [of pain] *in the period after the operation,* [being] *frequent infections and a palpable mass, this would suggest the presence of retained surgical bodies.*

I am in the basement.

Approximately 80% of cases diagnosed with RSB[s] *are those in which the number of declared materials was* [counted as] *correct at the end of the operation. Good communication inside the operating room is essential for minimal errors during surgery.*

Thank you very much for the presents. I also got 10 dollars.

Sponges are [the most common] *foreign bodies retained in* [humans] *after surgery, being located in body cavities such as the abdomen, pelvis and retroperitoneal space … RSB inside the abdominal cavity can produce … tumours that can raise suspicions for malignant mass, intra-abdominal abscess, obstructive ileus, intestinal perforation, gastrointestinal fistula, bleeding and can migrate transmurally.*

When we got home from Florida I saw the Shazam boxcar under the tree and it was light blue and red. The shirt is good.

The most commonly retained surgical items are sponges. Leaving surgical sponges [as well as other equipment is] *referred to as gossypiboma or textiloma.*

Today, a raisin fell up my nose.

2.

Dear Santa

An 84-year-old woman was admitted to hospital with weakness, lethargy and infectious secretions of the umbilicus. The patient had undergone hysterectomy 21 years before … The patient was … a candidate for laparotomy, which revealed a long gauze attached to a band and a metal ring in the umbilicus and hypogastric regions as well as a large abscess containing 200 ml of infectious secretions, severe adhesions of the intestines … [and] *an approximately 1 cm fistula … in the Ileum due to the foreign body.*

Mom wants me to write you a thankyou letter. I like N scale model trains now but I also like HO. Dad made me a train set that fits into the bottom bunk of my bunk beds. Thank you for the Santa Fe engine and the coal cars. The coal cars say Santa Fe on them and you can take out the coal that is plastic. I live in Santa Fe. They came from de Vargas Mall. Thank you for the Capsela and the Spacewarp. The new mall is Villa Linda on Rodeo Road. Gram and Gramp drove down this year with the old lawn mower in the trunk but forgot the spark plug in the basement.

One in every 1,000 [to] *1,500 intra-abdominal operations … occur*[s] *at least once per year in hospitals where 8,000* [to] *18,000 … surgeries are performed annually. We report a case of a forgotten Asepto bulb in the vagina following a robot-assisted total laparoscopic hysterectomy.*

I got 20 dollars from Gramma and I got 45s. I made a train tunnel from plaster of Paris and I played 'Tarzan Boy' by Baltimora and 'Break My Stride' by Matthew Wilder and 'One Night in Bangkok' by Murray Head and 'Puttin' on the Ritz' by Taco and 'Let's Go All the Way' by Sly Fox when I made the tunnel and I like hearing them many times to hear new things when I hear them again.

As soon as [clinicians] *saw her patient's C.T. scan … radiologists paged Dr. Anne Dembitzer, an internist at the Veterans Affairs Hospital in Palo Alto, California.*

The Santa Fe derailed inside the model tunnel. I helped Dad gather wood from the Park Plazas green belt to start a fire on Xmas Eve. Piñon pine smells good. We have a new chimney and a Kiva fireplace with two nichos. The New Mexico chimney is bigger than the Minnesota chimney and the bricks are new and yellow. You will be able get down it quickly. I also got 'Lean on Me' by Club Nouveau.

The patient … had consulted Dr. Dembitzer because of nausea and pain in his abdomen … This was the second clamp to be found inside the same patient. The first one, left after intestinal surgery … was found eight months after the operation and removed by the same surgeon who had left it. It caused an infection that made the patient ill. The second clamp … was left behind in the same operation as the first, but was somehow overlooked when the first was found … The patient would need yet another operation to take out the second clamp.

Dad got me fireworks from Ft Sumner because it did not take up much room in his minivan. The Santa Fe derailed because I put five ladyfingers in the Bangor & Aroostook potatoes boxcar behind the engine and lit the fuse with a match that I put in a glass of water and had the transformer on and it was running and that is where it exploded in the tunnel.

The New Mexico chimney has a flue that is easy to open and when you get there you can do it. Like Dad told me about when he was a kid in Billings, I look up into the Xmas tree and I see all the lights and it looks like a city with people and my friend Colin might come down next year. Annie is my dog and she chases rabbits on the green belt but cannot catch them. I like the smell of burning.

Three factors [stood] *out. Compared with patients who did not have objects left inside them, those who did were nine times as likely to have ... emergency surgery ... Disorgani*[s]*ation increases* [with complexity], *making it harder to keep track of sponges and equipment. The third factor was size: people who were heavy were more likely to have objects left behind than lean people, simply because there is more room for ... things.*

At the top of the chimney, Dad took pictures of the cardboard cut-out of the G scale Burlington steam engine with a real sunset so it was all black and because I wanted to win the *Model Railroader* picture contest but we left the lens cap in the picture by accident and we did not win because you could see it and they said so. I cut paper smoke out from construction paper and taped it to the smokestack so it looked real. It was thick.

The patient ... had the two clamps left behind [and] *suffered from pain, abscesses and septic shock, and, his lawyer said ... the infections and septic shock led to a stroke ... The original operation in which the instruments were left was an emergency procedure, and it was not the hospital's practice to count instruments, the lawyer said.*

Can you breathe thick smoke? Model trains and things can get down this new New Mexico chimney and I hope you and what you have can because I know that is what it must were. Mindy is in her room, and in the refrigerator are batteries and film but there is milk and a few shrimp and sauce.

3.

Dear St Nick

Hello again. I heard about the study where there were *60 potential cases in CRICO's administrative data base. Fifty-four were confirmed to involve a retained foreign body after surgery and to have the required medical records available.*

I am still into fireworks. This year, I asked you for another box of explosives and by accident I found it underneath my parents' bed around Thanksgiving before Xmas. When I came home from school before my parents got home I got the box out from underneath the bed and I smelled it and it smelled like fireworks.

Nick, *a 61-year-old female patient presented intermittent discomfort, pain, and serous discharge at the site of previous liposuction operation on the periumbilical area. The patient had undergone a liposuction surgery 10 years ago.*

I did this many times and then I planned to open the box to sneak a look even though I knew I should not and so I got scissors and Scotch tape and a sharp knife and I opened the box to see what was inside while my parents were not home.

Cases involved 61 retained foreign bodies … 69[%] *of cases involved sponges* [and] *31*[%] *involved instruments. No major bodily cavity was spared.* [54%] *of the foreign bodies were left in the abdomen or pelvis,* 22[%] *in the vagina, 7.4*[%] *in the thorax, and 17*[%] *elsewhere, including the spinal canal, face, brain, and extremities.*

It was fireworks and I was excited. I took them all out of the box. I had to lean under the bed to get the box.

No surgeon was responsible for more than one case.

Discomfort had started 9 years after the liposuction.

I picked up each firework and noted its label and I smelled them. The sky rockets just fit in the box and I saw that the brand of the fireworks was from Flaming Arrow Inc. of Albuquerque, New Mexico, and this was the same company where I had written a letter to and mailed it to them because I always wanted to know how to get fireworks in Santa Fe.

The objects were most often detected by radiography or computed tomography (67[%]*). Other retained objects (24*[%]*) were detected* *on physical examination or self-examination (particularly for objects left behind after vaginal procedures) or on reoperation (9[%]).*

You know I like fireworks? I think about them and I feel hot and see colours and then a lot of time passes before I notice that I am still thinking about fireworks. And I do not know that I do not move but then I remember that I feel like I am wearing a small shirt and it feels weird to move my arms. And sometimes I feel like it is night dark when I think of fireworks even though it is not dark.

Nick, there was also a time where *a thirty-year-old woman presented with gradually progressive abdominal distension and mild fever fifteen days after a caesarean operation. At admission, she was febrile. Clinical examination revealed an ill[-]defined, mildly tender, left lumbar swelling. Laboratory investigations showed ... leucocytosis with neutrophil predominance.*

And when I crawled under the bed to get the box I felt my belt loop caught on a screw and it was hard to reach my belt when I was under the bed getting the box of fireworks.

And then *ultrasonography revealed a large, mixed echogenic mass in the left lumbar region ... There were multiple speckled gas bubbles within the mass. At laparotomy, a*[n] ... *abscess surrounding a surgical sponge was found.*

I put all the fireworks back in the box the way they had been put in there from the beginning but I could not get them all to fit, and when I Scotch-taped up the box with the clear tape so that my parents would not know that I had opened it the box did not close all the way and I was scared.

A twenty-two-year-old man presented with left loin pain within two days of a nephrectomy. Clinical examination ... failed to reveal any abnormality. Plain and contrast enhanced C. T. scan showed a low-density focus suggestive of gas in the left renal fossa ... On interaction with ... surgeons, it was found ... that the operating surgeons had placed gel foam particles in the left renal bed to control intra-operative haemorrhage.

The box bulged now and it did not look right. When I eat steak, I like the taste of the fat when I chew it. And I am chewing.

Nick, I could not get all the fireworks back in the box. I lied to my parents that I did this when they asked me if I had done this and I felt hot and dizzy.

And they *discovered a folded, yellow rubber foreign body in the abdominal wall. The size of the rubber foreign body was about 1.0 × 9.0 cm.*

And I re-wrapped the present in Scotch tape and the same wrapping paper and put it back under the tree and hoped that they did not notice but they did. I want to look up when I write this but I can't because the air feels heavy and I feel dots and smoke so I will say goodbye because it feels like I have cotton balls in my sight and I want to barf like the time that the badger ate a half gallon of margarine at the cabin and got sick on the gate to the cookhouse.

To obtain [the] *cases, records* [were sought] *from all malpractice claims … involving retention of a surgical instrument*[s] *or sponge … filed between* [1] *January 1985 and* [1] *January 2001, with the Controlled Risk Insurance Company (CRICO), a malpractice insurer … A computeri*[s]*ed search of CRICO's … data base* [was done] *to identify potential cases.*

I went up to my parents' room a day later to check on the box and remembered that one sky rocket would not fit and I tried to fit it when I repacked the box. And I forgot it outside the box and underneath the bed. And now it is no longer underneath the bed when I just checked and I am chewing fat and I don't know where the sky rocket went.

4.

Dear S

I cannot tell if I am under my blankets or not, but it feels like I am in a made bed with all its sheets still tight like in the motels in Beach, North Dakota, and Glendive, Montana, that we stay at. It is the only time we eat McDonald's although Mom and Dad call it the golden arches to try and be sneaky so my sister and I do not know dinner and so it is a surprise.

S, as I mentioned in an earlier letter, *A 61-year-old female patient presented intermittent discomfort, pain and* [a] *serous discharge at the site of* [a] *previous liposuction operation on the periumbilical area. The patient had undergone a liposuction surgery 10 years ago.*

The new New Mexico chimney is big like I wrote about, but I have not heard from you. Dad said maybe it was starlings nesting above the damper, but I worry that you are up there and stuck. The chimney is square and I can imagine your beard boxed in around your chin and neck at the top of the new chimney. And your stomach and belt buckle pressed into a square tube and expanding like a database that I read about in *World* magazine for kids. And sometimes I forget about you or that you are up there.

... the umbilicus ... disappeared and serous discharge with symptoms of pain, itching and discomfort ... started 9 years after the liposuction. The patient had been treated with antibiotics and dressing at a local clinic ... her symptoms did not improve with treatment. She visited [an] *outpatient department ...* [and] *was referred for an ultrasound screening. The ... screening showed fluid collection at the umbilical area.*

The Happy Meals had a Grimace and Hamburglar eraser that you could stick on the end of a pencil but they came in a plastic wrapper that was hard to get open because it was placed under the cheeseburger and was oily.

The size of the fluid collection was about 1.3 × 1.3 × 3.5 cm.

I also got a French Fry Guy in a clear wrapper but I could not get it out and then Dad was driving the new Ford pickup and had to brake quickly and I fell off the stack of suitcases in the back of the truck and broke my nose.

The size of the rubber foreign body was ... 1.0 × 9.0 cm.

I was too afraid to tell my parents I had broken my nose.

I am looking up the new chimney and I can see what I think are boots? Did Christmas leave you behind? I'd forgotten about you again because Mom said I could use the cordless phone.

... *yellow rubber foreign body in the periumbilical area. The specimen was sent for biopsy and bacterial culture test. The pathology results suggested hyaline fibrotic tissue and necrotic amorphous material.*

It is nearly March and there are marks that look like waffle tread in the soot. Do you need the right shoes to get out of houses? I do not see a sack of toys beneath the boots, but there is something that looks like a dead banana leaf or what Dad said might be a colostomy bag or an XXXL tee-shirt. Can you breathe? Have your fingers and shoulder gone to sleep? Tingling like an electronic sandstorm?

The patient was a 35 year old ... female who had discharged from [cutaneous] *fistula* [and] ... *abdominal pains 5 months after* [C] *esarean section of her second child with Pfannenstiel incision. She was hospital*[s]*ed with ... anorexia, low grade fever ... f*[a]*ecal discharges and symptoms of partial bowel obstruction.*

If I play Betty Boo's 'Boo-mania', would that help? I need to call Nikos and Tim.

Can you breathe?

Subsequently, the umbilicus was … buried in the abdominal wall. We retracted the buried umbilicus and reconstructed [it].

It's March and Dad has put a cap on the new chimney so starlings and bats do not roost inside. If you are in there I can leave some biscochitos and horchata and some shrimp and shrimp sauce for you.

You have slipped inside my house to give me tame dynamite. I don't know where you are. If you die in my new chimney I don't know how to get you out, but your suit is red enough to keep you happy until next fall, right?

I need to call Rebecca because the fair at Villa Linda has the Zipper and we want to ride on it but I have to ask her out first.

In fistulography, there [was evidence] *of* [a] *fistula between* [the] *small intestine and skin with unusual gas pattern in bowels and retained gauze in terminal ileum. Findings of laparotomy were fistulas between caecum, terminal ileum and skin with* [severe] *intra-abdominal adhesions … The patient underwent entrolysis, terminal ileotomy and right hemicolectomy ... Ovaries, ureters and uterus were normal.*

Do you deliver toys because you want to or because you are expected to? I want things and because I want things I want more things and more model train boxcars and a second cheeseburger. I can see rainwater dripping down the inside of the chimney, but it was sunny today I think. I can't remember because I was on the cordless with Rebecca.

5.

Krist Kindl

My retinas, dead. Dark. And I am parked, not in hosannas, but in your subcutaneous blubber and on the admission that I am cuddling your liver like I do pillows in the night. Along the way, I'm amphibious. I have one arm up around your pancreas and the other is snaking a way down your colon and with a handful of bladder. It's hot, and I can feel it swell and release in tides of incoming brandy. There is a lot to say about sacks.

Suspended in aspic. How is it that I can breathe? My legs have punctured yours, and they wend around your trunks as an epiphyte would. The mistletoe kind. Did you listen to The Boss on your sleigh? Everybody knows Reagan got it wrong, but we didn't know any better then, and, since I was born in the USA, it is my right to litigate against why I am inside you, and have been all along and, failing that, I can shoot you and, in concert, re-litigate against you if you don't die. I didn't want just the one boxcar. I didn't want just three pencil erasure figures. I didn't want Rebecca or Tim or Nikos. I wanted things and boxcars and explosives.

Brain death occurred due to subarachnoid [haemorrhage] *in a 75-year-old … donor in another transplant cent*[re] … [the] *local transplant team harvested the* [liver] *and sent it to our cent*[re] *within nine hours … and the graft was transplanted to a 50-year-old patient. In the post-operative period … an increase in leukocyte count and fever were seen … There was a thin, long foreign body inside the anterior branch of the portal vein supplying this* [graft]. *Removal of the catheter by interventional radiology was* [considered] … *but found more difficult than its surgical removal … The portal vein was opened from an extra-anastomotic area … and a 10-F catheter piece, 5 cm long, was removed. The portal vein was closed …*

I press my face up between your lungs and nudge an eye as close to your skin as I can. Your breastplate is sharp. But, when I do this, I can see gossamer sutures of sunlight. Of altitude. I can see shadows of the bunting festooning your velvet. It's gauzy, and on the outside. And I am in. I am your caloric intake. I ate the holiday salami. I ate the limited-edition Kit-Kat. If I turn my head, I can look into the abyss of your blood, and it feels like it would be glacial blue. Capillaries and extension cords, plugged into the attic of what it is to be born. I'd kill for a turkey and butter sandwich. You can't eat a 7", no matter how you spin it.

A 27-year-old woman … presented with abdominal pain at 38 weeks' gestation. Her medical history included a Caesarean section 5 years before at another hospital … On examination, she had a mobile, obvious, firm, non-tender mass in the suprapubic area. During ultrasonography, an echoic mass … was detected. A 2,900-g healthy male infant with an Apgar score of 9 … was delivered. At the Caesarean … a piece of retained surgical towel was taken out …

And yet, it is a vast inner space here. Organs undulate from your laugh. And I am sustained, looking as I frequently do, down past the coupons and discount codes, past the catalogues, the wish-lists and the Ponzis that tilt just so. Santa, I can see for kilometres in here. Ages. There is no curvature, but there are things. And whatnot. I will be okay. I am commerce. And when you tilt me upside-down and jostle me like a snow globe, I can see coins, all the coins, falling onto children holding out for more electric trains.

California

'Dairy laborers, Vacaville. Cristero revolution.'

Gelatine-silver print from 4x5 negative, 1928. National Farm Bureau

purple martins violin
a man maker

braid   a well
humming age painters

fill   frame   bail
english   shush

donkey silenced
now belong   an order

despite ear   into
bird amused sisters

beast steeple
home time mirrors

'John Chong on the Rail road. At Vallejo near Sacramento'

Ektachrome commercial 7252 assemblage, 1978. Berkeley Art Museum/Pacific Film Archive

club   bell firefly
exercise dark

telescope   heels
peel dawn   black

alley rowing   machined
chronometers

nebulae away
rest legs   synthetics

botanic nose   bone
pine confinement

excellent ships
septum   to thousands

'Crenshaw High class of '76. TLM third row fifth from right'

800mm f/11 catadioptric panorama. California Historical Society (by donation)

brazen toms
conscript   queens

winding back   ward alfalfa
in state   curricula

permit nearsightedness
throaty   tornado

ghost gas   depend
calendars to brick

low   globes
bubble wrap

writ of pink   hammer
bingo jewels

'Portrait of Huddie "Leadbelly" Ledbetter, ca. 1940s.'

3x4 Series C Graflex with Cooke 2.5 lens. American Folklife Center

cheer led   tooth bop
yak   deflation

bearskin sale   pile
sunset   buttons ulcerate

libertarian function
quick night wrestling

wets   mandarin dream
chaparral   biome crazy

manzanita   coat cold
a gigantic bat   horse

wire   speechless manure
men boiled again

‘Gangster cameo (Polanski) cutting nose of J. J. Gittes’

Enlarged frame publicity still. Panaflex-X, 40 mm lens. Paramount Pictures

surf bang   savage
chess   bored groundwater

apricots register   decagons
jokes tire   funny sand

assaults   the midriffs
cardplayers finger

at metaphor   implicit
valentine   women vomit

a mailman   schnauzer
limits   double catholics

are   we is
buster keatons pigeon

'Frame 340.978.222.09 at 1.71 picoseconds'

Gatsometer 24, Exif metadata. 30 June 2012. Temecula Police Department, City of Temecula, CA

DD-cup halt   cakes gridlock
a raven's boot   stank amperes

municipal   candlepower
craps   redder jaguar

golgotha   valve
ethnicity elbows   jab

feldspar   to quickcrete
daddies   goat balance

a drive-thru   echolocation
fossil convoys   weed

tropospheric hills   find copper
speed-traps   ermine veal

'The Last Yahi: L-R: Sam Batwi, Dr. A. L. Kroeber, and Ishi (Southern Yana Indian)'

Eastman Kodak Hawk-eye No. 2. 4 x 5. Phoebe Hearst Museum of Anthropology. UC Berkeley

whippoorwills underdress   if magistrate
mountains snore   in

fields   escape rotation
ferret found   breeze

moon hides   caves become
suburban cassettes   old

industry rose   dates
deal in   wigwams

pierce onyx   edge
rustic   bambinos gin pi

granite chapters   podcast how
brooks pretzel   circulate law

'Holy smokin' cow! I had the Diablo Burger. Wow!'

Consumer 12d, male. Carl's Jr. rear advert, Scala Ad Manager.
Monterey-Salinas Transit

web-learning   byline
sketches monterey   incisor jack

spooks chew   weatherproofing
technique by   kipflers

slit ultramarine   tombola
centrifuge cattle   vis-a-vis frangipanis

of moon gas   clientele
curlicue   long division

vultures obey   let   magazines
coagulate   alphabet

zeros pocket   crowdfund
404 missing   fuel caps

'Majik Seven – Live in Los Angeles / Utah Saints – Lost Vagueness'

Cut up concert bill, letter. 120 gm honey foil. Hewlett-Packard Mopier 320 System

peak-a-boo   chapters blip
uno   with message

photos of   photographs
parallax wince   at   cuticles tilt

fog border   zen-somethings
guidebooks   shill

exacting   blanks
dworkins latest   vasectomy

bubblewraps   bivalve
pornography   the hinged

dos   conveyance moog
twins skip   double dutch

Case Study

I

In 1984, the Kingston Grove Toy & Novelty Co. of Perth Amboy, New Jersey, emerged from bankruptcy administration with Harmon Clayton Killebrew Jr – nicknamed 'The Killer' and noteworthy for accomplishments in modernising intermodal shipping and trucking logistics – installed as CEO.

Kingston & Co. began as a manufacturer of flash paper and film processing equipment in 1917, and, by 1922, meeting high demands ushered in by the Roaring 20s, expanded into novelties, noisemakers and magic tricks. The company prospered with a variety of toy and gimcrack lines. In 1958, it produced a home run commercial hit with its answer to the hugely successful Lincoln Logs via the Lady Loggs toy construction kits.

The Lady Loggs range offered market distinction in its brightly coloured parts, and it included a novel array of plastic componentry to construct model swimming pools and convertible automobiles during play. Sales of Lady Loggs sets peaked with a robust 39.8M revenue in 1977, and sharply decreased over the next 5 years – the dawn of the PacMan era – until its discontinuance in 1982. The company filed for bankruptcy in 1983, and again in 1984.

II

In early 1986, Kingston's product development team green-lit the Baby CreepFace doll in response to the lucrative Cabbage Patch Kids line produced by Coleco Inc. and the sophomoric but popular line of Garbage Pail Kids products from legendary baseball trading cards manufacturer Topps Inc. The Baby CreepFace's retail distinction was that it would appeal to diverse children in a light-hearted, fun and earnest attempt, for this specialised sector, to identify themselves in a nationally popular toy.

Prototype testing began during the winter of 1984 in the small metropolitan markets of Portland, ME; Tacoma, WA; Duluth, MN; Tucson, AZ; and Macon, GA. These markets were selected for varied population-base testing, unique climates, and because their predominantly blue-collar economies were perceived to represent ideal locations for future Baby CreepFace sales.

By early 1986 – after extensive interrogation of the 1980 census and target testing in day cares and kindergartens – 5 versions of the Baby CreepFace were identified as the likeliest to generate revenue in small to mid-sized, predominantly manufacturing-led economies. The Kingston marketing team found that, beyond the standard Anglo doll, additional alternative models would reflect research and fit their acceptable sampling plan. 'Your only handicap is being alone' was selected as the toy line's marketing hook, and a trademark for its exclusive use was applied for in late 1985.

III

Kingston faced significant engineering requirements in refurbishing equipment last used to cut, dye and apply polyurethane baths to its wooden Lady Loggs assemblage. Plastic components for the dolls required injection stamping machinery, flues, hoses and polymer vats. Moulds once used in the manufacture of concave swimming pool parts could be repurposed to fashion convex craniums and torsos and, more specifically, double for some superior epiphysis and plural scapulae representation required for alternative models.

Although dormant for over 4 years, the bankruptcy protection court deemed Kingston's extant infrastructure an asset for its fit-out to produce the Baby CreepFace in adherence to Jidoka principles and cost-conscious insourcing. Kingston emerged from receivership with a modest 26.8M line of credit from State Street Bank & Trust in Peabody, MA, and creditors were buoyed by new revenue opportunities in the big-box retail bonanza occurring at the time. After Kingston entered into agreements with Wal-Mart Stores Inc., Dollar General, Pamida Partners and Skaggs Alpha Beta supermarkets, its credit line more than tripled to 85.4M.

Kingston brokered an abandoned lot sale of 1785 gigalitres of a plastics solution from Malinski Chemical LLC of Terre Haute, IN.

Its original purpose was for use in the manufacture of chainsaw cowlings, ride-on mower guards and industrial pruners. However, during normal operation, the machines caused too high a level of vibration fatigue, posing a significant safety hazard. The chemical asset was liquidated after Malinski lost a lawsuit brought upon it by the family of a golf course groundskeeper in Huntsville, AL, who had been fatally decapitated by faulty machinery manufactured from its product. Kingston acquired the lot at $0.27 on the dollar.

IV

When combined with a rubber additive and refined with industrial milk solids, the chemical proved to have sufficient integrity to mould plastic doll componentry estimated to withstand organic play in a wide range of climates as well as to produce a lifelike skin texture. Additionally, the compound responded well to dyes, and Kingston's production plans continued apace to accommodate the toy line's full marketing plan. With limited capital, there was no room for error or product-environment research on getting Baby CreepFace effectively to market.

Repurposing defunct equipment last used for Lady Loggs production proved more challenging than initially calculated. As Kingston's Perth Amboy plant sat dormant, significant infestations of eastern gray squirrel (*Sciurus carolinensis*) and barn swallow (*Hirundo rustica*) colonies compromised its complex injection and plumbing network. Investing in new equipment and vacuum flushing its salvageable piping with solvents posed to be a costly proposition for Kingston: resulting in the delay of Baby CreepFace's market penetration, forfeiting Year 0 buying season leverage and/or unforeseen capital expenditure on plant repair.

V

Killebrew opted to sacrifice 60% off Kingston's initial non-white dye mixture to flush its hoses and reservoirs free from an encrustation of pest faeces and carcasses, and to recycle that mixture for production. Kingston's line of credit was revised downwards to 59.9M, but with an option for an additional 9M in commercial paper.

Share prices held at expected levels, and the consumer outlook remained rosy. Killebrew appeared on *Donahue* and the new *The Oprah Winfrey Show* in autumn 1986, in both placements appearing with 'child actor' [sic] and *Diff'rent Strokes* situation-comedy star Gary Coleman, a Baby CreepFace product champion.

VI

In early winter 1986, production at last began. Killebrew further appeared on the CNN and CSPAN nightlies touting the advent. The dolls were manufactured from unblemished pre-mix and the previously used quantity, with 100% of upstream throughput shipped to Dollar General warehouses in Murfreesboro, TN, and Pine Bluff, AR, just in time for the Christmas merchandising season. USD $29.99 was the price point for the standard Baby CreepFace, with the first alternative model escalated to USD $34.99 due to greater complexity in capturing realism in the product's embodiment (a tenet of Kingston's branding vision). Q4 1986 sales beat expectations, albeit modestly, and production of hue mixtures across all alternative models began in early 1987.

An 'undetected mixture error', as later reported in *The Wall Street Journal* and *Wealth Insights*, affecting all Year 0 units produced, complicated Kingston's plans for full line expansion.

VII

By mid-March 1987, it was discovered that warmer springtime temperatures and an increased daily dew point caused dye in the plastics to deteriorate, resulting in the alternative model dolls becoming a dark purple, sugar beet colour. This unexpected product behaviour was first noticed at a Dollar General location in Natchitoches, LA. There, Kingston's retail placement remained in direct sun for the entirety of business hours, and with the outlet's untinted glazing amplifying luminosity onto its Baby CreepFace presence.

Kingston filed suit against Dollar General franchisee Vernon Smathers & Partners Inc. for negligence via wrongful asset treatment, but the 15th Judicial District Court in Lafayette Parish, LA, dismissed the claim by stating that 'All of Louisiana's children must be able to build immediate product agency, and window display is a primary channel for that acculturation process'.

VIII

By late spring 1987, Dollar General outlets throughout Alabama, Florida, Kentucky, Mississippi, Texas, the Carolinas and various Ozark locations pulled Baby CreepFace stock. Killebrew ordered the recall of all Year 0 units on 17 May 1987 to staunch brand collateral damage. Concurrently, alternative model Year 1 units had shipped with great fanfare to Pamida and Skaggs distribution centres in Barstow, CA, and Pueblo, CO. Sales rebounded over Q3 1987.

Kingston touted a deluxe alternative model yield itemised in its 1988 prospectus – reflecting a recently identified, soon viable Baby CreepFace market in anticipation of 1990 census data. Shares gained an 18% market cap position from industry buzz. In addition to the confirmed Bermuda short, camouflage vest, Hammer pant and sombrero inclusions for the deluxe model, talks began with Reebok International Limited to license a leisure-, foot- and winterwear accoutrement suite for the new product's value addition.

Kingston deftly crafted its relationship with Reebok at a significant discount, assuring its partner that cross-branding would influence whole-of-family purchasing instinct as reciprocity for its diminished equity stake in the deluxe Baby CreepFace. Said Killebrew in an *Adweek* spotlight about the joint venture, 'Our dolls for children will, by extension, sell golf and swimwear to their parents, not to mention badminton and lacrosse gear to older siblings'.

IX

In October of 1987, retail complaints began to surface in Nogales, AZ; Las Cruces, NM; and in Fresno-Modesto, CA locations that alternative Baby CreepFace models suffered from structural integrity malfunctions. Customers discovered that when exposed to sustained sunlight, the plastic composition began to photo-decompose, rendering most facial features and digits indistinguishable, greatly affecting play. A number of reports from the Laredo and El Paso, TX markets noted skin rash generation and clear or white vesicles forming on operators' skin during product use.

Q4 earnings projections were swiftly revised, and shareholders became understandably spooked by the revelations. Kingston's credit was again geared downwards to a 12.7M draw. Killebrew ordered the publication of a full-page, apologetic statement in over 100 small to mid-sized market newspapers of record ∞ "Kingston Grove Toy & Novelty Co. of Perth Amboy, NJ, is baloney, and has never existed. You've probably already googled 'Baby CreepFace doll' and found no results, because there never was such a toy, nor were there ever any Lady Loggs."

X

But maybe, now, you are somewhat surprised to learn that this has *not been* true, that Mr MacCarter has been an untrustworthy narrator, and that, like him … but never mind him, really … your puberty was hunted by the pugnacious miasma that is hysteria capitalism, and the apex predators that feed it. Surprised, maybe, at being *not* surprised, if allured, that such a product *could have* been conceived this callously.

The retailers, publications and TV shows noted do exist, or once did. Cabbage Patch and Garbage Pail Kids cards sold untold container-loads. Coleco Inc. scampered for bankruptcy protection because it could not manufacture its Cabbage Patch Kids *fast enough* in the 1980s, such was the pitch of consumer zeal.

Indeed, a man named Harmon Clayton Killebrew Jr. – nicknamed 'The Killer' – did exist. Me. But I was in the pro baseball racket, and I don't know squat about supply chains, petroleum-based products, sweatpants for dolls, market segmentation or what children in Dixieland or all those places out past Albuquerque want. Wasn't Bo Diddley a deputy sheriff in Valencia County, NM, in the '70s? Ask him.

'We're currently deceased, complicating the thrust of this piece.'

XI

However, I did once hit a 520-foot home run into the upper decks of Metropolitan Stadium in Bloomington, MN. That blast was 37 feet longer than Hank 'The Hammer' Aaron's longest – I touched it right good – and you know how Stanley Kirk Burrell got his moniker, I trust.

The Old Met was demolished in 1981, and the Mall of America – largest retail space on Earth – now serves A&W root beer, soft tacos and friend cheese curds where it once did Grain Belt lager and franks. The home plate, where I stood and swung then, is commemorated by a modest plaque in 1 of the 570 retail outlets – won't tell you which one.

The original seat where my longest ever homer landed is bolted to a wall high above the mall's indoor amusement park flume ride – the kind of thrill where kids get showered in fake rain and splash – exactly where, at the elevation and to the distance, I parked it from home plate in 1967. Hint: they sell toys.

Epilogue

Cyan: 0%, Magenta: 69%, Yellow: 100%, Key: 6%

US Coast Guard u-turned to Pier Thirty-nine
        August DeMont co-produced daughter number one
                Carol DeMont was her name

Jack Ricketts and Al Maloux were painting a bridge
        August co-produced a second daughter named Marilyn DeMont
                Jack and Al watched Marilyn exit a car

Marilyn did not speak
        August requested that Marilyn jump
                August was thirty-seven and spoke

Marilyn scaled metre-high rail on Bay side
        Jack and Al were painting a bridge
                Jack and Al watched Marilyn jump

Marilyn jumped
        Irving Morrow selected colour
                Marilyn and August did not speak as they jumped

August left note on car seat
        Marilyn was little and did not read
                Jack and Al watched August jump

August wrote note
        Jack and Al painted colour on steel
                Marilyn and August did not *jump*

Carolyn Downes became more with Carolyn DeMont
        Steel got born in Bethlehem, Pennsylvania
                August and Marilyn dived in sequence

Car was 1942 Plymouth sedan
    Auto belongs to Mrs AC DeMont
        4356 Twenty-sixth street, San Francisco

    I and my daughter have—

August jumped on 23 July 1945
    Golden Gate Bridge International Orange
        Carolyn recounted, *I knew it, I knew it*

August did
    Irving felt colour was highly pleasing
        Carol was Measles in bed on 23 July 1945

Marilyn and August swept into Pacific and got eaten
    Measles are Golden Gate Bridge International Orange
        Jack and Al were painting on 23 July 1945

Date in Potsdam Harry Truman spoke of Fat Man and Little Boy
    August co-produced daughter number two
        Jack and Al watched a car

Marilyn did not speak
    Jack and Al were
        Carolyn found little at Pier Thirty-nine

Facts rely on International Date Line
    Regret sums 220 feet between South Tower and Bay
        August did earthquake-proof lifts in towers for living

Acknowledgements

I would like to thank Jessica L Wilkinson for her insightful introduction, and for offering significant feedback on the development of this book. Too, thank you to Lisa Gorton for sharp insights on making this a better collection.

Sam Cooney, John Kinsella, Emmett Stinson and Donna Ward also read drafts and offered support over the years, to which I am grateful. Pascalle Burton, thank you for your encouragement.

Big thank you to Terri-ann White and Upswell Publishing for believing in this book and making it real. Kelly Somers, good catches.

Some of the writing in this collection first appeared in *The Lifted Brow, Overland, The Victorian Writer* and *Westerly*. Excerpts of some pieces also appeared in *Sputnik's Cousin* (Transit Lounge, 2014) and *California Sweet* (Five Islands Press, 2019).

'Fat Chance' is non-fiction, 'California Suite' is an exercise in reverse-ekphrasis, 'Gossypiboma' is a memoir and science-based bricolage and 'Case Study' is satire that is not yet all-the-way non-fiction, but will be eventually, and is heavily influenced by personal experiences pursuing business degrees.

This collection was written between 2012 and 2023; no artificial intelligence was used in its creation. Thank you to the worldwide journalists, first responders and witnesses that felt motivated to report.

'Gossypiboma' incorporates excerpted portions of:

'Retained Surgical Foreign Bodies after Surgery' by V Zejnullahu, B Bicaj, V Zejnullahu and A Hamza

'Twenty Years with a Retained Foreign Body after Hysterectomy: A Case Report' by M Mashhadi and M Shahabinejad

'To forget is human: the case of the retained bulb' by K Sakhel and J Hines

'Forgotten Surgical Tools "Uncommon but Dangerous"' by D Grady

'Imaging features of gossypiboma: report of two cases' by S Prasad, A Krishnan, J Limdi and T Patankar

'Buried umbilicus with inflammation due to retained rubber foreign body after liposuction: A case report' by J Kim, J Shin, S Roh, S Chang and N Lee

'Risk Factors for Retained Instruments and Sponges after Surgery' by A Gawande, D Studdert, E Orav, T Brennan and M Zinner

'Imaging features of gossypiboma: report of two cases' by S Prasad, A Krishnan, J Limdi and T Patankar

'Buried umbilicus with inflammation due to retained rubber foreign body after liposuction: A case report' by J Kim, J Shin, S Roh, S Chang and N Lee

'Buried umbilicus with inflammation due to retained rubber foreign body after liposuction' by J Kim, J Shin, S Roh, S Chang and N Lee

'Textiloma, migration of retained long gauze from abdominal cavity to intestine' by H Govarjin, M Talebianfar, F Fattahi and M Akbari

'Retained Foreign Body in Transplanted Liver' by C Kayaalp, S Kırmızı, R Kutlu, M Yagci, B Isik and S Yilmaz

'A foreign body (gossypiboma) in pregnancy: first report of a case' by C Dane, M Yayla and B Dane

About Upswell

Upswell Publishing was established in 2021 by Terri-ann White as a not-for-profit press. A perceived gap in the market for distinctive literary works in fiction, poetry and narrative non-fiction was the motivation. In her years as a bookseller, writer and then publisher, Terri-ann has maintained a watch on literary books and the way they insinuate themselves into a cultural space and are then located within our literary and cultural inheritance. She is interested in making books to last: books with the potential to still be noticed, and noted, after decades and thus be ripe to influence new literary histories.

About this typeface

Book designer Becky Chilcott chose Foundry Origin not only as a strong, carefully considered, and dependable typeface, but also to honour her late friend and mentor, type designer Freda Sack, who oversaw the project. Designed by Freda's long-standing colleague, Stuart de Rozario, much like Upswell Publishing, Foundry Origin was created out of the desire to say something new.